This journal is dedicated to
Executive Assistants everywhere...
You truly keep the wheels rolling on the bus!

Our success depends on you!

Please take a moment to leave feedback on Amazon.com
And THANK YOU for your purchase!

Copyright © 2014 by Blue Icon Studio
ALL RIGHTS RESERVED

All quotations remain the intellectual property of their respective originators.
We do not assert any claim of copyright for individual quotations.
All use of quotations is done under the fair use copyright principal.

Designed by M.L. Baldwin

is a registered trademark of Blue Icon Studio
Blue Icon Studio, Lexington, Virginia, USA.

> The secret of success is to do the common things uncommonly well.
>
> ~ *John D. Rockefeller*

> It is an immutable law in business that words are words, explanations are explanations, promises are promises but only performance is reality.
>
> ~ *Harold Geneen*

No one is more cherished in this world than someone who lightens the burden of another. Thank you.

~ *Author Unknown*

> It's easy to make a buck. It's a lot tougher to make a difference.
>
> ~ *Tom Brokaw*

> The world is moved along, not only by the mighty shoves of its heroes, but also by the aggregate of tiny pushes of each honest worker.
>
> ~ *Helen Keller*

Oh, I'm not bossy;
I've been blessed
with an
administrative gift.

> Always be nice to secretaries. They are the real gatekeepers in the world.
> ~ *Anthony J. D'Angelo*

> I can no other answer make, but, thanks, and thanks.
>
> ~ *William Shakespeare*

Act as if what you do makes a difference. It does.

~ William James

What would you attempt to do if you knew you would not fail?

~ *Robert Schuller*

There's only one corner of the universe you can be certain of improving, and that's your own self.

~ Aldous Huxley

> Something that has always puzzled me all my life is why, when I am in special need of help, the good deed is usually done by somebody on whom I have no claim.
>
> *~ William Feather*

> You give but little
> when you give of
> your possessions.
> It is when you give
> of yourself that you
> truly give.
>
> ~ *Khalil Gibran*

Instead of counting your days, make your days count.

~ *Author Unknown*

> The only gift is a portion of thyself.
>
> ~ Ralph Waldo Emerson

Improvement begins with I.

~ Arnold Glasow

To be successful, you have to have your heart in your business, and your business in your heart.

~ *Thomas Watson, Sr.*

Successful people are always looking for opportunities to help others. Unsuccessful people are always asking "What's in it for me?"

~ *Brian Tracy*

> The greatest good you can do for another is not just to share your riches but to reveal to him his own.
>
> ~ Benjamin Disraeli

There are no secrets to success. It is the result of preparation, hard work, and learning from failure.

~ Colin L. Powell

> I would maintain that thanks are the highest form of thought, and that gratitude is happiness doubled by wonder.
>
> ~ G.K. Chesterton

As soon as you sit
down to a cup of
hot coffee, your
boss will ask you
to do something
which will last until
the coffee is cold.

~ *Author Unknown*

Be nice or I'll send you to a meeting!

The difference between a successful person and others is not a lack of strength, not a lack of knowledge, but rather a lack of will.

~ *Vince Lombardi*

Professionalism is
a frame of mind,
not a paycheck.

~ Cecil Castle

> Let no one ever come to you without leaving better and happier.
>
> ~ *Mother Teresa*

Make the

workmanship

surpass the

materials.

~ Ovid

> Gratitude is the memory of the heart.
>
> ~ Jean Baptiste Massieu

How wonderful it is that nobody need wait a single moment before starting to improve the world.

~ Anne Frank

Usefulness is
happiness, and...
all other things are
but incidental.

~ *Lydia Maria Child*

Appreciation is a wonderful thing. It makes what is excellent in others belong to us as well.

~ *Voltaire*

> People will forget what you said, people will forget what you did, but they will never forget how you made them feel..
>
> ~ *Unknown*

Success is simply a matter of luck. Ask any failure.

~ *Earl Nightingale*

You're no good
unless you are a
good assistant;
and if you are,
you're too good to
be an assistant.

~ *Martin H. Fischer*

> Excellence is doing ordinary things extraordinarily well.
>
> ~ *John W. Gardner*

> Successful and unsuccessful people do not vary greatly in their abilities. They vary in their desires to reach their potential.
>
> ~ *John Maxwell*

> If you have much, give of your wealth; if you have little, give of your heart.
>
> ~ *Arabian Proverb*

> Dealing with people is probably the biggest problem you face, especially if you are in business. Yes, and that is also true if you are a housewife, architect or engineer.
>
> ~ *Dale Carnegie*

> What a person believes is not as important as how a person believes.
>
> ~ Timothy Virkkala

> There are so many men who can figure costs, and so few who can measure values.
>
> ~ *Author Unknown*

> You must be the change you wish to see in the world.
>
> ~ Mahatma Gandhi

It's nice to be important, but it's more important to be nice.

~ Author Unknown

> Wise are those who learn that the bottom line doesn't always have to be their top priority.
>
> ~ William Arthur Ward

> The secret of
> success is
> consistency of
> purpose.
>
> ~ *Benjamin Disraeli*

Desire is the key to motivation, but it's the determination and commitment to an unrelenting pursuit of your goal - a commitment to excellence - that will enable you to attain the success you seek.

~ *Mario Andretti*

Work as if you own the company and soon you just might.

~ *Mike Dolan*

Next to excellence

is the appreciation

of it.

~ William Makepeace

> Great opportunities to help others seldom come, but small ones surround us every day.
>
> ~ Sally Koch

> Always bear in mind that your own resolution to success is more important than any other one thing.
>
> ~ *Abraham Lincoln*

Hire character.

Train skill.

~ *Peter Schutz*

> Do not wait for leaders; do it alone, person to person.
>
> ~ *Mother Teresa*

> Success usually comes to those who are too busy to be looking for it.
>
> ~ Henry David Thoreau

> Not only must we be good, but we must also be good for something.
>
> ~ Henry David Thoreau

www.ingramcontent.com/pod-product-compliance
Lightning Source LLC
Chambersburg PA
CBHW081729170526
45167CB00009B/3762